Original title:
Interstellar Irony

Copyright © 2025 Creative Arts Management OÜ
All rights reserved.

Author: Juliette Kensington
ISBN HARDBACK: 978-1-80567-875-5
ISBN PAPERBACK: 978-1-80567-996-7

Cosmic Whispers of Deceit

In the void, stars laugh and tease,
Secrets twinkling on a cosmic breeze.
Planets spin with merry lies,
While moons wink from velvet skies.

Galaxies dance, a cheeky waltz,
Stumbling over dark matter faults.
Comets crash with mischievous glow,
Leaving trails of what we don't know.

Gravity's Playful Grip

Oh, gravity, don't be so sly,
You pull my socks to the nearby sky.
Planets tumble, one by one,
Chasing each other just for fun.

Rockets laugh and fly awry,
Defying forces with a zippy sigh.
Like toddlers in a space-time field,
They dance and spin, never yield.

Black Holes and Broken Dreams

Down the throat of a black hole's grin,
Swallowed hopes and a cosmic spin.
They say if you reach the event's core,
You'll find lost socks and tales galore.

Time bends here, a playful jibe,
Where dreams dissolve like quantum vibe.
Astronauts chuckle, chasing fate,
With a map that leads to a cafe straight.

Winks from the Universe

Look up, my friend, at the starry sky,
The universe winks, oh me, oh my!
Jupiter giggles, Saturn spins a tune,
While Mars plays tricks with a dust-filled croon.

Nebula clouds puff up and smile,
As shooting stars dash in playful style.
Each twinkle whispers, a cheeky jest,
In this cosmic dance, we're all just guests.

Celestial Contradictions

Stars twinkle like they know the truth,
Yet they hide behind a cosmic sleuth.
Planets spin in chaotic dance,
While comets laugh at their own mischance.

Galaxies swirl in a whirl of jest,
Caught in a game, we all are a quest.
Black holes munch on the light of day,
While flatterers think they'll find a way.

Dark Matter Shenanigans

In the void where shadows play,
Dark matter giggles and leads us astray.
Gravity's pranks spin us around,
While we search for the lost, never found.

Neutrinos waltz with invisible style,
As we ponder the void, wondering all the while.
The universe jokes in a cryptic way,
Leaving us puzzled day after day.

Holograms of Hope

Dreams projected on a cosmic screen,
Holograms dance like they're playful and keen.
Wishing upon a tech-based star,
While we giggle from up here, afar.

The universe winks with a sly little grin,
As we ponder the chances we've missed or won in.
Waves of laughter ripple through space,
In a virtual realm, it's a humorous race.

The Comedic Canvas of Night

Night paints laughter across the sky,
As meteors race, they zoom and fly.
Constellations form silly shapes,
While we chuckle at what the cosmos scrapes.

The moon holds secrets cloaked in glee,
While the sun's bright mug makes a mockery.
As we gaze up, we can't help but see,
The comedy show of infinity.

Nebulae of Nonsense

In a cloud of colors, stars play peek-a-boo,
Planets wobble, swirling in silly cue.
Gravity chuckles, pulling dreams back tight,
While comets giggle, zipping off in flight.

Space cats float, chasing cosmic yarn,
Asteroids dance with a twinkle and charm.
Galactic giggles echo through the void,
As space unfolds, a stage of the absurd enjoyed.

Planetary Punchlines

Why did Mars refuse to cross the street?
It's afraid of Earthlings with nothing to eat!
Jupiter jokes, with moons in each hand,
While Saturn's rings play in a cosmic band.

Pluto pouts, longing for a comeback,
Says, "I'm still here, no need for the flak!"
As meteors laugh at their speed and their fate,
The universe finds humor—don't underestimate!

Laughter Between Galaxies

A star with a sparkle sent a joke to the sun,
But it was too hot—oh, what a run!
Neptune snickers as it sips on some gas,
While black holes munch on time—what a class!

The Andromedan dance takes cosmic delight,
Twisting and swirling, they're quite out of sight.
In the vastness, humor expands with the light,
Creating a laughter that lasts through the night.

The Absurdity of Astral Journeys

On a rocket ship made of banana peels,
Travelers giggle at their clumsy heels.
Cosmic clowns juggle stars with swift grace,
Wishing on wishes, they float through space.

A photon stops to take a selfie so bright,
While black holes trap mirrors—what a sight!
In the waltz of the cosmos, they chaotically spin,
Finding the joy where the journey begins.

Orbiting Dilemmas

In a galaxy far and wide,
Lost socks drift with cosmic pride.
Stars play hide and seek in space,
While comets chuckle, keep the pace.

Asteroids argue, whose turn to glide?
While black holes quip, 'We tackle with pride'
Gravity giggles, pulling us in,
As planets spin, wearing a grin.

A Dance of Dust and Paradox

Stardust twirls in a cosmic dance,
While meteors waltz, taking a chance.
A paradox lost, now found in the void,
While light-years laugh, feeling overjoyed.

Mars sends a postcard: 'I'm red and I'm hot!'
Venus replies, 'Well, I'm quite the plot.'
Galaxies giggle, in a spiral embrace,
As gravity hugs, leaving no trace.

Saturn's Rings of Sarcasm

Saturn spins with rings of gold,
Joking 'I'm stunting', feeling bold.
Uranus winks, 'I'm just a tease',
While moons roll their eyes, 'Can we just freeze?'

Jupiter grumbles, 'I'm king of the ball',
But the tiny asteroids barely recall.
As nebulae giggle, painting the scene,
Stars poke their heads in, 'What does it mean?'

Quantum Quips

Quantum leaps with a jumpy jest,
Particles play hide and seek, the best.
Entangled in laughter, they twist and twirl,
While photons giggle, flashing a swirl.

Wave-particle paradox, who's in the lead?
Both sides chuckle; they're up to the speed.
As universes ponder the cosmic display,
Time winks at space: 'We'll join the play.'

Whims of Distant Worlds

Planets dance in circles tight,
Yet one forgot to turn off the light.
Stars twinkle like they know the score,
While comets bump and ask for more.

Gravity's a prankster, light as a feather,
Pulling us close like it's some great tether.
Aliens giggle at our silly plight,
Waving goodbye as we try to take flight.

Stellar Whimsy

In a galaxy far, folks lose their car,
Searching black holes, they wonder and spar.
Time loops and wiggles, a cosmic charade,
While space cows chew their intergalactic hay.

Saturn lost its ring in a game of blink,
Uranus rolled over, which made them all think.
Asteroids play tag, and planets make bets,
At the end of the day, it's not that complex.

Cosmic Comedy

Nebulae giggle at our earthly fears,
Jokes lost in translation across the light years.
Mars throws a party, sends out invites,
But Earthlings show late—oh, those long flights!

Stars in their orbits get dizzy and spin,
Galactic Follies, let the fun begin!
Wormholes twist smiles, while black holes play pranks,
As distant worlds laugh at our earthly flanks.

Diagrams of Delay

Spaceships scheduled, but time's gone awry,
Engineers puzzled as clocks all fly by.
Launchpads are ready, yet rockets just yawn,
The universe chuckles as dawn starts to fawn.

Emails in space take a month to arrive,
While stardust trails sparkle, making us thrive.
Napping in voids, the astronauts jest,
In a cosmos where silly is surely the best.

Orbiting Sarcasm

In space where stars post memes,
Gravity laughs at our dreams.
Planets spin with a cheeky grin,
While astronauts lose their helmets with a spin.

Orbiting jokes at light-year speeds,
Cosmic puns plant silly seeds.
Black holes snicker at our plight,
As we scramble to find our flight.

Asteroids chuckle in their dance,
While we endlessly search for a chance.
Galaxies wink with knowing glee,
Mocking our hopes, carefree and free.

Even comets trail laughter bright,
As they zoom past in the night.
The universe plays a grand jest,
In the cosmos, we're all just guests.

A Laugh Beyond Time

Tick-tock says the cosmic clock,
Wormholes wave and tell us to rock.
Time pulls pranks with every tick,
Sending us back for one more kick.

Chrononauts trip on paradox trails,
Where logic falters and humor prevails.
Laughing at the age-old chase,
As time takes us for a wild race.

Dimensions twist with a playful tease,
And spacetime folds like a piece of cheese.
We tumble forth in the great unknown,
Laughing at what we can't condone.

A giggle echoes from years long past,
As we grasp for wisdom—so vast.
Through time's vast expanse, hear the mirth,
In every second, we find our worth.

Distant Echoes of Truth

Whispers float from light-years away,
Tales of the universe's funky play.
Stars gossip in a twinkling hue,
Sharing your secrets, they know it's true.

Astrophysicists scratch their heads,
Wondering why their logic treads.
With every answer out of reach,
Cosmic jests are the ones they teach.

Gravity waves carry chuckles clear,
Jovial forces we hold so dear.
Planets giggle on their merry way,
As we ponder what they may say.

In the end, humor's the key,
To unlock the cosmos' mystery.
So laugh with the stars, let truth unfurl,
In every riddle lies a swirl.

Anomaly in the Cosmos

Oh, what's that shape in the void we see?
A cosmic blunder, a sight most free.
Comets crash with a clumsy spin,
While aliens poke at their own skin.

Hyperspace has its own wild quirks,
Bending the rules, it slyly lurks.
Wormholes smile as they give us a fright,
Guiding us through the oddest night.

Scientists chuckle at the bizarre,
Measuring laughter from afar.
For every theory that seems so right,
There's always a glitch that steals the light.

It's a dance of absurdities, bright and bold,
In this vast theater, watch tales unfold.
So we embrace the strange, the wacky we toast,
In this anomaly, humor's the host.

When Comets Laugh

A comet zooms with a wink,
'Thought I was lost, but I think!'
Through cosmic lanes, it sways,
In a ballet of starry rays.

Asteroids chuckle, tripping along,
'This dance is right; that's all wrong!'
Planets roll their eyes in delight,
As meteors make a silly flight.

Black holes giggle in the void,
'We swallow stars; they get overjoyed!'
Nebulas puff their wispy pride,
While galaxies play tag side by side.

So if you gaze at the night,
And hear a comet's chuckling flight,
Remember space is a jest,
Where silence brings the loudest fest.

Timeless Reflections

In the mirror of cosmic sands,
Reflections twist, as nature plans.
Time jumps, but watches with glee,
As seconds dance, oh so carefree.

A star declares, 'I'm old and wise!'
While a baby sun winks with surprise.
Asteroids stuck in a time warp,
Mimic laughs in a merry sort.

Light-years travel, but what's the rush?
When all that's real is a playful hush.
Comets tease like jokes of yore,
With echoes that always ask for more.

Each twinkle brings a silly smile,
As gravity pulls at cosmic style.
The universe whispers funny schemes,
In the vastness of our giggling dreams.

Galactic Misunderstandings

A satellite called out to a star,
'Hey, do you know where we are?'
The star just shone with a bright light,
'You got the map? It's quite a sight!'

Planets argue about who's more round,
While moons spin tales of lost and found.
'Think I'm larger!' one said with pride,
'Though gravity knows it's all a ride.'

Aliens ponder, 'What's life, though?'
Their pets eat stardust, putting on a show.
They laugh, 'Our cats are now stars!'
While dogs bark at distant quasars.

In this theatre of the absurd,
Misunderstandings spread like birds.
The universe laughs, 'Oh what a play!'
In the great cosmic cabaret, hooray!

The Irony of Infinite Space

In a sky that stretches wide and far,
Yet we struggle to find a car.
The universe spins in wavy lines,
While we can't keep track of our own signs.

Stars count wishes, they're all on hold,
As we fret 'bout dreams that grow cold.
A black hole yells, 'I'm full tonight!'
While we wonder about dinner's bite.

Galaxies mock, spinning in glee,
'What's the hurry? Just enjoy the free!'
Time is a loop, but we take the train,
Chasing sunsets while it simply rains.

In endless space, a cosmic jest,
We struggle hard but hardly rest.
So when you gaze at the stars up high,
Just remember to laugh; it's worth a try!

Lightyears of Laughter

In a galaxy far, far away,
Stars giggle in their playful sway.
Comets zoom with jokes untold,
While black holes munch on cosmic gold.

The moons dance in their quirky suits,
Jupiter juggles asteroids like flutes.
Saturn's rings twirl in a cheeky spin,
As aliens laugh, let the fun begin!

Planets play hide and seek all day,
Mars claims it always wins the game play.
But Earth chuckles, full of delight,
Knowing it's wrong, but oh, what a sight!

So lightyears stretch with giggles absurd,
In a universe where joy's assured.
When stardust sprinkles on our dreams,
Laughter echoes in cosmic themes.

The Universe's Riddles

Why did the star go to the show?
To learn the secrets that the universe knows.
A neutron walks into a quark bloom,
And the hydrogen laughs, filling the room.

Light beams cross with a cheeky grin,
While the rogue planets spin and spin.
Galaxies waltz in a comical race,
As time trips on, just losing its place.

Asteroids play peekaboo with fate,
While the sun winks, never late.
A riddle wrapped in a cosmic jest,
Is the universe here just to keep us blessed?

With every twinkle, a punchline intended,
As far-out theories keep us befriended.
Here in the void where wonders collide,
Laughter's the answer, no need to hide!

Gravity's Mistaken Embrace

Gravity just wants a hug, it seems,
Pulling us in with its heavy dreams.
But when we trip over our own two feet,
We laugh hard while trying to stand on the street.

A meteorite falls, it trips on its way,
"Oops!" it exclaims, "Not today, hooray!"
Planets roll around in clumsy delight,
As they swirl and tumble into the night.

Stars create chaos while trying to align,
"Why's it so hard?" they joke, "What's the line?"
Gravity chuckles, pulling them close,
In a tangled dance, who knows who's the host?

So here we float in this silly ballet,
As celestial bodies go on their way.
With every fall and every embrace,
The universe laughs, a whimsical space.

Constellations of Confusion

In the night sky, shapes play tricks,
A bear looks like a bunch of sticks.
Orion shouts, "I'm a space knight!"
While Taurus sighs, "I'm lost in the night!"

Planets argue on who's more bright,
While the moon rolls its eyes with delight.
"I cycle through phases, watch me glow!"
But the stars all say, "Oh, steal the show!"

Constellations mix up their lines,
As scripts from the cosmos produce funny signs.
A lion's roar inside a fish tale,
This cosmic circus can't fail to prevail!

Each twinkle's a bump in this dizzy dance,
With comets who dive like they've lost their pants.
So celebrate the chaos, let laughter beam,
In the sky where dreams and starlight gleam!

Celestial Chimeras

In a galaxy far, quite absurd,
A comet sips tea, how very unheard.
The planets all dance, in mismatched pairs,
While black holes steal socks, without any cares.

Space whales sing tunes, of lost cosmic socks,
And meteors giggle, like chickens in blocks.
Asteroids wear hats, quite dapper they look,
While aliens read from a baffling book.

In the cosmos, such chaos, the fun never stops,
Nebulae tie bows, as gravity flops.
Stars play hide and seek, as they twinkle and shine,
Mocking the orbits, with flavors divine.

So launch your dreams, beyond the mere sight,
In this wacky expanse, everything's light.
With laughter and whimsy, the cosmos unfolds,
Their secrets a jest, in the way they are told.

Out of Orbit Expectation

Expectations soar like a rocket's great height,
Yet planets just yawn, with dull cosmic light.
A Martian forgot, it was map day today,
He's lost in his thoughts, in a comical way.

Jupiter's storms spin tales of old storms,
While Saturn's new rings host bizarre little swarms.
Astrologers puzzled by stars in a tiff,
Claiming the moon's just a galactic grift.

Your GPS? It just flickers and hums,
The universe chuckles, as lost wanderers come.
With each twist and turn, we laugh at the jest,
For space has its humor, a cosmic request.

As orbits collide in a playful embrace,
Let's ride on the waves of this vast outer space.
For plans oft go wrong, like a jester's bright plan,
The punchline awaits in the orbit we scan.

The Cosmic Game

Gravity's a player, always in style,
With the sun as the dealer, our fate's on a dial.
Asteroids roll dice, while comets draw hands,
In this game of stars, no one quite understands.

Neptune bets blue, while Venus plays round,
Each planet's a card, in this poker compound.
Jovial Saturn spins fables of fate,
As planets all grumble, they're losing their weight.

But the universe giggles, with whispers of fate,
As black holes consume what they claim as great.
The rules shift and change like a playful charade,
For what is a loss, if laughter's the trade?

So join in the fun, there's no need to fear,
In this galactic game, we all persevere.
With snickers and chuckles, the cosmos will sing,
For laughter is cosmic; it's the best kind of bling.

Stars' Silent Laughter

In silence they twinkle, the stars share a jest,
While planets just wobble, in their bright little nest.
Galaxies giggle, in spirals galore,
Whispering secrets from realms we explore.

A star once pondered, 'Is this all a show?'
As meteors whizzed by, with a comic glow.
While beings on Earth argue, mired in strife,
The cosmos just chuckles at their daily life.

A cosmic orchestra plays tunes unheard,
With planets as players, in harmony stirred.
Yet, through all the chaos, the universe winks,
Its humor unearthly, as odd as it thinks.

So look to the heavens, let your cares go afar,
For in this vast expanse, we're just comets in a jar.
With laughter entwined, let joy be the call,
In the grand scheme of things, we're not so small.

The Edge of Absurdity

Galaxy's spinning, what a sight,
Stars all laughing, day and night.
Planets wobble, can't keep still,
Space-time giggles, what a thrill.

Aliens dance with glowing grace,
Tripping on gravity's funny face.
Comets tailing like jokes on a roll,
In this vast emptiness, chuckles console.

Asteroids tumble, what a mess,
Knocking on black holes, they just guess.
Quasars crack up, shining bright,
Comedy in chaos, pure delight.

Every lightyear, laughter grows,
Cosmic humor, who really knows?
Witty echoes from nebulae vast,
A universe of jest, unsurpassed.

Laughter Between Galaxies

A light year's worth of silly pranks,
Floating jokes in cosmic banks.
Wormholes whisper, secrets tease,
Laughter bubbles in cosmic breeze.

Martians trading puns for fun,
Orbiting joy like a stellar run.
Supernovae burst in glee,
Explosive bursts of comedy.

Stars wear hats, moon a tie,
Celestial beings passing by.
Meteors zoom with witty flair,
Galactic giggles fill the air.

In the void, we share our jokes,
Amidst the swirling cosmic folks.
Bright constellations grinning wide,
In the arms of space, we bide.

Rifts in Stellar Truth

Black holes joke with gravity's friends,
Pulling at laughter that never ends.
Comedians drifting in space-time's play,
Telling tales that twist and sway.

Stars collide in comic fights,
Sharing headlines of meteor nights.
Neutron stars with quirky charm,
Spinning yarns, they spread the warm.

The universe's prankster flair,
Joking light-years, who'd dare compare?
Light from supernovas takes a bow,
As irony fades, yet laughs still wow.

Through cosmic rifts, the truth unwinds,
Laughter lingers, space always finds.
What's real or fake? It's hard to tell,
In humor's grasp, we all dwell.

The Dark Matter of Humor

In shadows where bright comets glide,
Lurks the laughter we try to hide.
Neutrinos tickle, dancing near,
The dark matter's a jester here.

Saturn's rings with giggles spin,
Witty whispers in the din.
Uranus rolls with cosmic jokes,
Even in silence, humor pokes.

Gravity pulls at punchlines tight,
While echoes bounce in the cold, dark night.
Comedy veiled in the universe wide,
Where laughter swims, secrets confide.

So look to the stars, see what they do,
The universe chuckles, a big cosmic crew.
In the vastness, we find our place,
The dark matter of humor, a warm embrace.

Cosmic Threads of Irony

In the vastness where comets play,
Planets giggle, stars sway,
Time's a jester with tricks to spin,
What's lost in space, we find within.

Galaxies twirl in a cosmic dance,
Black holes hide their ironic glance,
Chasing light, we miss the jest,
While aliens laugh at our quest.

Nebulas puff in a colorful jest,
"Look at those humans, they think they're the best!"
Yet through the void, they float and drape,
Cluelessly wrapped in their own tape.

Cosmic irony's a curious thing,
Count the chuckles that comets bring,
In the silence where laughter grows,
Who knew the universe has funny bones?

Specks of Humor in the Infinite

In endless voids, tiny jokes reside,
Each quasar winks, with laughter inside,
Fleeting moments, timelines bend,
A cosmic punchline around the bend.

Planets wobble with comic glee,
Orbiting futures none can foresee,
Starlight sparkles, bright and bold,
Making jest of all we're told.

Asteroids tumble, giggling loud,
In the silence of space, no crowd,
Galactic chuckles fill the air,
As we ponder life, unaware.

In the universe's sprawling grasp,
Every twinkle, a cosmic gasp,
Amidst the vastness, we find our way,
Laughing at the games stars play.

Beyond the Event Horizon

Beyond the depths where light can't flee,
Lurks a humor, dark and free,
Gravity's pull, a jesting threat,
Where losing your way is the best bet.

Singularity swirls in a playful whirl,
Spinning tales of time, it gives a twirl,
"Step right up, if you dare to try,
Lose your watch, but give me a high!"

Photons reach out but fall in a trance,
Caught in the grip of cosmic romance,
A laugh echoes back from a void so deep,
"Keep your secrets, let the light weep!"

Beyond the edge, where logic bends,
The cosmos plays, and reality mends,
For in this space, with nothing to see,
Jokes float around, wild and free.

Stars' Wry Smiles

Stars twinkle with a mischievous grin,
Winking at all who dare to begin,
Chasing dreams through the dark expanse,
Leading lost souls in a cosmic dance.

In the night sky, a satirical plot,
While we scramble, they laugh a lot,
Cosmic jesters, with humor profound,
In their laughter, wisdom is found.

Constellations sketch their own tale,
Showing us paths that funny prevail,
Mapping out jesters' realms above,
Reminding us humor is the real love.

So let us gaze at the brilliant light,
Finding smiles in the vast night,
For every star that twinkles high,
Holds a giggle amid the sky.

Reflections in Stellar Streams

In a galaxy far, lights blink and play,
Stars hold secrets, they giggle all day.
Planets dance round, like kids on a spree,
Yet they rarely notice how funny they be.

Astronauts float with snacks in their hand,
Lost in the void, they hardly can stand.
A comet zooms by, wearing a hat,
While meteors laugh, 'Oh, imagine that!'

Black holes are jesters, they swallow with flair,
Pulling in laughter from everywhere.
Wormholes, the punchline, a twist in the tale,
Turned outraged voyagers into a snail.

Yet as we gaze at this cosmic parade,
We tumble through jokes that the universe made.
For in these vast realms of uncharted delight,
Humor's the beacon, shining so bright.

Gravity's Grin

Falling through space, with snacks in a sack,
Gravity pulls, but I've got no knack.
You'd think I'd float free, but no such luck,
I'm tethered to earth—what a cosmic chuck!

The moon's in on it, a giant cheese wheel,
Pretending it's rock, but what a good deal.
Each swing with the tides, a playful tease,
"Come dance with me, human! I'll squeeze!"

Without gravity's tug, I'd surely be lost,
But oh, the fun of this roundabout toss.
A dance here, a twirl, then plummet with glee,
Just another stunt in this cosmic spree!.

Yet even in orbit, there's laughter to find,
As planets collide with the silliest mind.
This volatile joy, hurling without end,
In the universe's play, we all just pretend.

Time's Twisted Sense of Humor

Time plays tricks with a wink and a nudge,
It skips like a stone, it spills like a fudge.
Moments go flying, like kids on the swings,
Racing through seconds, oh, the joy it brings.

"Wait—was that Monday?" I ponder aloud,
But time just erupts, the joker, so proud.
Tick-tocks keep laughing, they're out of control,
A countdown to chaos, a whimsical stroll.

With clocks on the wall, all staring in glee,
They giggle and snicker, 'Just wait and see!'
Years turn like pages in a weird novel,
Every moment we chase just dissolves with a squabble.

So here's to the time that plays hide and seek,
With a tickle of laughter, it's always so cheek!
Between here and there, it's a slapstick show,
In the grand cosmic comedy, let's join in the flow.

Nova's Provocation

A nova erupts with a wink and a flare,
Exploding in laughter—do stars really care?
With a flash of surprise, they throw cosmic pies,
To black holes, aghast, with wide-open eyes.

"Oh, look at me shine!" the novas all shout,
As they bicker and boast, in a starlit bout.
"A burst from a beam? What a marvelous sting,
Hand me that laughter—let's see how it sings!"

Crumbling planets roll with a giggly quake,
While supernova's humor makes galaxies shake.
This stellar comedy of chaos and light,
Is the punchline of dawn, a miraculous sight!

So here's to the sparks that ignite with a laugh,
In the cosmic banquet, we're all just a half,
Join in the twinkle, ride the wave of jest,
In this universe grand, it's humor that's best!

Fractured Fables of Time

In a space where clocks run slow,
A turtle raced a comet's glow.
The turtle cheered, 'I'm winning now!'
While comet's tail vowed, 'I'll take a bow.'

A spaceship lost in a game of hide,
Found a wormhole where potatoes cried.
'I'm just passing through,' said the spud,
As stars giggled, swirling in a dud.

A wise old alien raised a toast,
To an Earthling who thought he'd boast.
'Your feet are big, but take a look,
You can't even read a starry book!'

So time flips round like a silly chip,
Cosmic laughs in a paradox trip.
One moment a king, next a ghost in line,
What a riot, this galactic design!

Where Stars Wince

A planet danced with two left feet,
While comets groaned to a funky beat.
Stars rolled their eyes with a cosmic sigh,
'When did planets lose the reason why?'

A black hole birthed a curious joke,
Spitting stars like a soda folk.
'What's the punchline?' asked a bright new sun,
'You'll never know, it's just too fun!'

In a dim-lit bar where asteroids play,
One asked the sun, 'Why don't you stay?'
The sun grinned wide, 'I'm too hot to hold,'
While the moon laughed, 'You're just too old!'

Yet as they joked through the cosmic whirl,
In a galaxy filled with twist and twirl,
All the worlds share a silly cheer,
For timing's a joke when you've nothing to fear!

Mirth in the Milky Way

In the depths of the Milky Way's dance,
Frogs took flight, while cows in a prance.
Galaxies giggled, 'What a grand sight!'
As gravity flopped on a taco night.

A spaceship filled with clumsies galore,
Flipped a pancake, then opened the door.
'Why does it sizzle?' cried out a whale,
As laughter drifted on a comet's trail.

Stars twinkled bright, donning hats with flair,
Saying, 'Did you see that alien's hair?'
Saturn chuckled, 'Well, I have some rings,
But that style, my friend, what a wild thing!'

Through cosmic pranks and astral fun,
The universe spins, and joy has begun.
In a realm where irony takes a stroll,
Mirth echoes wide, feeding every soul!

Tales from the Dark Side

Once there lived a shadowy grin,
Who claimed to be the king of sin.
With jokes so dark, they tickled the night,
While light itself let out a fright.

A rogue star blurted, 'I'm lost in a maze,'
To which the black holes offered a gaze.
'Join us, dear friend, for a dance of woe,
Where even the dark can put on a show!'

One comet got stuck in a loop of mirth,
Swearing it was the craziest thing on Earth.
'Gravity's off, and I can't seem to land,'
While moons around laughed, completely unmanned.

So if you wander down the abyss,
Remember the hugs and the cosmic kiss.
For even in darkness, giggles can hide,
Among tales that shimmer on the dark side.

Celestial Contradictions

Stars so bright, yet cold as ice,
They twinkle down, oh what a price.
Planets dance in endless waltz,
In circles round, without a pulse.

Light-years away, we send a call,
Yet time moves slow, it takes its fall.
We wave to moons that never seen,
And laugh at comets' silly sheen.

Galaxies collide, but it's so neat,
A cosmic mess, a grand old feat.
While we sit here, on our small rock,
The universe giggles at our clock.

Black holes suck, then let us go,
Like cosmic clowns putting on a show.
In vastness wide, we seek a friend,
But time and space just love to bend.

The Universe Fools Us

We search for life in a far-off place,
But all we find is empty space.
A signal sent, then lost in waves,
The universe chuckles, how it misbehaves.

The sun shines bright, yet casts a chill,
We build our dreams, it bends our will.
Gravity's jokes, a pulling prank,
We float and flounder, a cosmic tank.

Asteroids zoom, like kids at play,
Yet we prepare for doomsday's sway.
With telescopes wide, we search the skies,
Only to find our own surprise.

In darkened voids, where laughter hides,
The cosmos spins, while science guides.
Yet here we sit, with papers stacked,
The universe laughs, "Get back on track!"

Lost in the Void

Drifting through a boundless sea,
Stars as friends, yet lonely me.
We map the skies, chart every zone,
But gravity's pull always feels like home.

Spaceships zoom, we raise a cheer,
Then floored by aliens—oh dear, oh dear!
We seek contact, they play hide and seek,
Galactic pranks; they think it's chic.

Time ticks on in a strange ballet,
We laugh and cry in this cosmic play.
Supernova smiles and black holes frown,
While we just spin, around and down.

In our quest for answers that seem so close,
The universe winks, it loves to boast.
We're lost in thoughts, with irony rife,
As space shows us the humor in life.

Cosmic Jesters at Play

Comets race, wearing strange hats,
Aliens joke 'bout our silly spats.
Asteroids laugh as they take a stroll,
While we all search for some distant goal.

Saturn's rings make a perfect stage,
Where nothing seems to age or rage.
Meteors giggle, crashing by,
While we pretend we can touch the sky.

The Milky Way spins, a dance so sleek,
Planets grunt as they take a peek.
We wave to stars that just don't care,
In this vast cosmos of cosmic flair.

So here we stand, in this cosmic joke,
With every twist, the universe pokes.
We smile and nod, lost in the fray,
As time and space have their fun today.

Starry Ironies Unveiled

In cosmic realms where laughter glows,
Asteroids dance in oversized toes.
Space cows moo in zero gravity,
While comets giggle with glee, you see.

A Martian finds a space-time map,
But it leads to a joke, a cosmic trap.
Stars twinkle with a wink so sly,
As robots chuckle, oh me, oh my!

Moon rocks hum a silly tune,
Saturn wears a grand balloon.
Galaxies swirl in playful hues,
As gravity trips on its own shoes.

Through telescopes, we spy the jest,
In every quasar, a punchline blessed.
The universe giggles, a comedic spree,
In this vast theater, all are free.

Parallax Perspectives

A star blinked twice, a cosmic wink,
While black holes ponder, do they sink?
Planets tease each other's spins,
And light-years laugh at life's odd wins.

Uranus grins like a jester bold,
As the Sun tells stories that never get old.
Nebulas puff with colors bright,
Each one with jokes that spark delight.

While satellites get tangled in laughs,
Distances shrink, like cosmic giraffes.
In this dance of light and mirth,
Every orbit shares a chuckle's birth.

Fade into twilight, where echoes play,
Galactic giggles are on display.
In physics' whimsy, irony reigns,
As humor travels through space's lanes.

Quantum Quips

A cat's in a box, it's in and it's out,
Quantum jokes leave us all in doubt.
Entangled laughter twists and turns,
In every corner, the cosmos churns.

Particles giggle like kids on a swing,
As waves of wit begin to ring.
Heisenberg's here, with a smile so bright,
Uncertainty wrapped in a comedic light.

Dark matter hides with a chuckle or two,
As physicists scratch heads, what can we do?
Time folds in laughter, bending the night,
While quarks and leptons share the delight.

In the void, where silence is loud,
Mirrors crack jokes, beneath a cloud.
The universe winks, both strange and wise,
In quantum realms, humor never dies.

Intergalactic Jest

In a galaxy far, where laughter flows,
Aliens wear socks, with mismatched toes.
Spaceships zoom with squeaky toys,
While cosmic dust hides playful ploys.

A supernova bursts, but look and see,
It's just a cosmic party, let it be!
Stars watch with bemused, sparkling eyes,
As meteors come in with silly cries.

On distant moons where time does twist,
Life forms craft irony not to be missed.
Black holes snicker, pulling jokes unkind,
While satellites orbit with laughter in mind.

In every supercluster, tales unfold,
Of humor in space that will never grow old.
Galactic jesters shine bright and free,
In the vastness of space, what a sight to see!

Reflections of Cosmic Laughter

In a universe so vast and bright,
Stars giggle in the dead of night.
Planets spin with a wink and grin,
Mocking the chaos, they twirl and spin.

Comets zoom with a comet's flair,
Hair though wild, without a care.
Galaxies swirl in a cosmic joke,
Tickling the void with each little poke.

Black holes guffaw as they suck things in,
While light beams dance, they just can't win.
A star sneezes, causing a flare,
Scattering dust all over the air.

In this cosmic jest, we float along,
Joined in laughter, a universal song.
So tip your hat to the starlit night,
For in this chaos, we find delight.

A Comedy of Orbits

In a ballet of planets, they twist and swirl,
Every moon with an exaggerated twirl.
Mars chuckles at Earth's busy race,
While Venus preens with a sultry grace.

Asteroids prank with their rocky toss,
Dancing around, they show who's boss.
Jupiter's storms roar with delight,
Laughing at Saturn's rings, so tight.

The sun takes jabs from planets nearby,
'Oh, why so hot?' it winks from the sky.
As comets chase tails of stardust dreams,
The universe glimmers with whimsical beams.

Each rotation and wobble tells a tale,
Of cosmic humor that will prevail.
In this grand play of celestial fun,
Who knew space could be so well-run?

Nebulous Contrasts

In wispy clouds where stars collide,
Nebulas laugh, their colors wide.
A pink puff tickles a blue-hued burst,
Creating art with a cosmic thirst.

Stars play hide and seek in the mist,
With giggles that none can resist.
While dark matter prances, unseen,
Making the cosmos quite the scene.

Quasars shout with a vocal flame,
Challenging silence to a cheeky game.
Planets peek through galactic haze,
Bewildered by all the dust's antics and plays.

As vision fades in the light of night,
The universe chuckles with pure delight.
For in these contrasts, laughter is found,
A harmony rich, where joy doth abound.

Play of Celestial Bodies

A satellite winks, then takes a spin,
While meteors laugh, 'Let the games begin!'
Nebulas twirl in vibrant display,
Dancing around like clouds of sway.

Galactic clowns in their bands of light,
Playing tricks on the endless night.
Stars pull silly faces, glowing so bright,
As lightyears crumble into pure delight.

Wormholes giggle, they're never the same,
Each jump through space is a wild game.
Astrophysics can't grasp their quirky ways,
For laughter's lost in the cosmic maze.

Among these bodies, a whimsical spree,
Where humor and wonder run wild and free.
So carry this joy through the stellar tide,
In the universe's jest, forever we bide.

Celestial Curiosities

In a cosmic dance, stars collide,
Yet here on Earth, we fuss and bide.
Aliens laugh with popcorn in hand,
While we search for life in our own sand.

Planets spin on a whim so grand,
But we trip on shoelaces and misplace our band.
Gravity tugs, but we jump so high,
Trying to touch that sweet, velvet sky.

Black holes devour with a grin so wide,
But our lunch gets stolen on the merry ride.
Falling through space with socks on our feet,
A universe vast, just a quirky seat.

Galaxies swirling, a peppy parade,
Who knew that stardust would be this charade?
Between the stars, a joke is spun,
While on Earth, we quarrel over who won.

Starlit Ironies

Comets flash by like jokes in the night,
While we miss the punchline, try hard to write.
Between the void, there's giggles untold,
As we scribble our wishes on bright yellow gold.

Aliens intrigued by our silly ways,
Decide to take notes through laughter-filled days.
Watching us struggle to find sensical lore,
While they sip moonlight and dream evermore.

Meteors fall with a charismatic flair,
But our wishes fizzle, lost in thin air.
Gravity grins as we trip and we slide,
In the galaxy's circus, we awkwardly glide.

A wink from the cosmos, a chuckle so bright,
Stars wink back at our speculative plight.
Yet here on this planet of push and of shove,
We spin in circles, looking for love.

Galactic Playfulness

Planets juggle, their orbits a game,
While we debate who's the wisest of name.
Laughter echoes through the asteroid belt,
As we ponder the thoughts that we've never felt.

Constellations come alive with a jest,
While we fill our schedules, never at rest.
Black holes chuckle at our frantic race,
As we dash to the finish, but lose our pace.

In the vacuum, joy is an endless ride,
While we spill coffee, our dreams we confide.
The universe twirls like a mischievous sprite,
As we try to shine, but end up in fright.

Stars sparkle like sequins, a dazzling trance,
While we trip over shadows, miss our own dance.
Yet in the chaos, there's solace to find,
In the laughter of cosmos, we're perfectly blind.

The Absurdity of Existence

In realms where logic takes a vacation,
We ponder existence with great admiration.
Philosophers debate through the light of the moon,
While squirrels critique them, they'll talk soon.

Monkeys on asteroids, sipping on tea,
Watch us ponder the meaning of life in a spree.
They chuckle as we trip over cosmic fate,
While they swing through the stars, it's never too late.

Dimensions twist in a dance so bizarre,
While we miss the bus, and gaze at a star.
The universe grins, with a knowing glance,
While we contemplate fate, forgetting to dance.

In the end, amidst chaos and glee,
Stars keep on twinkling; we sip our tea.
Absurdity reigns; isn't it clear?
Life's nothing but laughter, so let's give a cheer!

The Ironic Silence of Expanse

In endless voids where shadows blink,
The silence screams, or so we think.
Stars twinkle softly, donning a grin,
As comets crash, yet no one's in.

Astronauts float in giggling glee,
A cosmic joke, just wait and see.
With every orbit, chaos reigns,
Yet space ignores our petty pains.

A satellite spins with a spin of fate,
While planets dance a wobbly gait.
In short supply, they jest and tease,
As gravity does what it believes.

And so in silence, laughter grows,
While Earth thinks it knows how it flows.
Forever trapped in cosmic play,
The universe winks, "You're in my sway!"

Celestial Whispers

A rogue asteroid hums a tune,
While space dust flirts with a silver moon.
Galaxies giggle in spirals tight,
As rockets blunder, avoiding the light.

Stars gossip softly about our fate,
"Look at those humans, they're always late!"
Comets joke, "We'll crash OH so soon!"
Meanwhile, black holes take us for a boon.

A spacetime riddle wrapped in a tease,
The cosmos laughs with an ease to please.
While time stretches, it plays tricks pure,
Forget your worries, that's the allure!

So next you gaze at the twinkling skies,
Remember, dear friend, the stars are wise.
In this grand ballet of cosmic sway,
It's all a jest—just dancers at play!

Cosmic Paradox

In a strange realm where logic bends,
The universe mocks, yet still pretends.
Gravity's a prankster, pulling you near,
While paradoxes twirl with a sneer.

A light-year's journey seems quite absurd,
As aliens laugh without a word.
Time bends, just a playful jest,
As we chase shadows on this cosmic quest.

Planets collide, oh what a sight!
Two blunders dance in a clumsy flight.
Stars spin tales of their distant kin,
While dark matter snickers, "Where have you been?"

So join the jest in this twisty place,
Where irony orbits in the vast space.
With comets and quasars singing a song,
The truth is silly, can't go wrong!

The Stars Laugh Back

Beneath the glow of cosmic dreams,
The stars conspire with their beams.
They plot and snicker at our plight,
As we scamper through the endless night.

Planets wobble in their dress,
In a dance of chaos, pure ridiculousness.
"Humans are funny," they twinkle bright,
As we keep searching for cosmic light.

With every wish upon a star,
They chuckle softly, "How bizarre!"
Nebulas swirl, a colorful prank,
While universes giggle in the cosmic bank.

So laugh with the stars, they're full of humor,
In this grand theatre, we're mere consumers.
Drawn to the light, we'll never outsmart,
The universe rolls with laughter at heart!

Stellar Sarcasm

In the realm of stars so bright,
We search for wisdom, yet it's light.
Aliens laugh at our silly plight,
Claiming Earthlings are a comical sight.

Planets twirl in a waltz so grand,
But time takes its toll, nothing goes as planned.
Gravity pulls, yet we misunderstand,
We trip and fall on cosmic sand.

Asteroids wink as they dance in bliss,
While we fumble about, lost in abyss.
In the vastness, humor's the sweetest kiss,
The universe chuckles, and we can't resist.

So next time you gaze into the night,
Remember the stars in their endless flight.
They're laughing at us with pure delight,
A cosmic jest, a silly sight.

The Space Between Laughter

In the vacuum, where echoes fade,
Gravity bends the joke we played.
We're trying to soar, but we're stuck, delayed,
While black holes snicker, and thus they stayed.

Our rockets sputter, dreams take a dive,
We think we're smart, oh how we strive!
But comets zoom past, so fast they arrive,
While we wave back, feeling very alive.

Galaxies spin, chaos is the key,
Yet we stumble 'round like it's a spree.
Alien tourists take selfies with glee,
While we're just lost, like a wandering bee.

So laugh with the cosmos, it's wise and free,
In the space between laughter, who are we?
Just tiny beings, silly as can be,
Floating in jokes of vast mystery.

Cosmic Slip-ups

Navigating stars with a map upside down,
We drift through the void with a bit of a frown.
Aliens gather, not a soul from our town,
Whispering secrets of our cosmic renown.

Our spacecraft's motto, 'To infinity and fail',
As we launch into orbit, we seldom prevail.
The stars share a giggle, a sarcastic tale,
While we sing tunes of an epic detail.

Astrology calls while we're failing at fate,
We blame the moon as it laughs at our state.
The universe rolls its celestial weight,
We dance in the darkness, it's far too late.

With each cosmic blunder, we brighten the night,
While faraway planets chuckle with delight.
In the silence of space, there's joy in the flight,
As we slip and we slide into humorous night.

Stars that Never Align

We chart our course with starry-eyed dreams,
Yet planets conspire with their well-laid schemes.
Asteroids giggle, plotting contrary beams,
Directing our path away from those themes.

We think we've found answers in cosmic embrace,
But the universe nods, it's a silly chase.
The constellations conspire to leave no trace,
As we wander in circles, lost in disgrace.

Supernovae boast of their brilliant light,
While we mix up the day with the dazzling night.
Comets whiz past with mischievous delight,
As we scratch our heads, lost in our blight.

Yet laughter echoes through the vast, dark expanse,
Inviting us all to a cosmic dance.
So let's not worry about fate's circumstance,
For even in chaos, there's room for a chance.

Galactic Misunderstandings

The aliens thought we'd bring them peace,
Instead, we sent them our favorite cheese.
They built a shrine to dairy delight,
While we all laughed at their curious plight.

A spaceship lost its way in space,
Took a wrong turn, a very wrong place.
They landed on a giant marshmallow,
Bounced around like a cheerful fellow.

A signal we sent for a cosmic chat,
They answered back with a sleepy cat.
Now 'Meow' is the universal tongue,
And all our galactic songs are sung.

In the end, we toast with a drink,
To the quirks of space, oh how we think!
Lost in laughter, across the stars,
Galactic giggles, no matter how far.

Nebulae of Deceit

In swirling clouds of vibrant hues,
The stars play peek-a-boo, making news.
A comet promised to make a show,
But fizzled out, just like a soda blow.

A rogue planet thought it was so grand,
Claimed to rule over all the land.
But it tripped on a cosmic banana peel,
Now everyone can see how it feels.

Aliens plotted to steal our air,
But it turns out they really just wanted hair.
They left with wigs and a sassy grin,
Who knew that fashion was where to begin?

So let's raise a glass to their fate,
In this universe, we celebrate.
For every twist, a laugh to greet,
In nebulae, we find the sweet.

When Light Bends

They said light bends, just like a straw,
But when it tried, it caused great awe.
It wrapped around planets like a snake,
Kidding us all with every mistake.

A star tried to shine, oh so bright,
But got lost in the middle of night.
Dressed up in shadows, it played a game,
Sending night owls wild, what a shame!

A distant sun sent a wink our way,
But missed its target, oh what a day!
It hit a comet splitting apart,
Now it's a ball that's lost its heart.

So when light bends, don't take it to heart,
It's all in the fun, just a cosmic art.
For in these quirks, we find delight,
Chasing the stars, making merry all night.

Shadows of the Infinite

In shadows thick, the secrets play,
Hiding truths in a funny way.
A black hole laughed, it spun so fast,
It swallowed jokes and let none last.

A twinkling star tried to take a bow,
But stumbled into a nebula, wow!
Spinning tales of cosmic grace,
Yet ended up in a gas cloud's embrace.

A whisper floated across the void,
Of UFOs missing, oh so paranoid.
They searched for home where they belong,
Only to find they'd parked too long!

So here's to the shadows, casting their charm,
In the vast expanse, they mean no harm.
With laughter echoing through space's dome,
Each silly story feels just like home.

www.ingramcontent.com/pod-product-compliance
Lightning Source LLC
Chambersburg PA
CBHW071821160426
43209CB00003B/153